Caribou Hide

Two Stories of Life on the Land

Written and Illustrated by Alfred Masuzumi

Raven Rock Publishing
Yellowknife, NT

About the Author:

 Alfred Masuzumi of Fort Good Hope, Northwest Territories, was born at Big Rock, a traditional fish camp on the east channel of the Mackenzie River Delta, some fifty miles east of Inuvik. Alfred's parents had gone to the Delta to trap muskrats.

Educated at the Federal Day School in Fort Good Hope and residential schools in Aklavik and Inuvik, Alfred has worked in many different areas. He did research for the Indian Brotherhood in the early years of the Dene Nation; he has worked as a linguist; also as a trapper. He has done research and held workshops on traditional knowledge. He is a carver, an artist, and a printmaker. This is his first book.

Dogs

In the Spring of 1968, George Barnaby and I were trapping at an historical lake called E Fe No T'o Tue, meaning 'Carried Caribou Head Across Lake.' It was about seventy miles west of Colville Lake, a small village of about seventy people in the Northwest Territories. We were running short of groceries. We discussed the situation and decided that I should go for groceries as I had more dogs and could make it back in reasonable time.

I had seven dogs and they all had individual names. The lead dog was Puppy. The second dog, Shubin, was my special one. He was the size of two dogs. At normal standing, when I was holding onto his collar, it was at waist height. Whenever I was travelling inland and going up a hill, I would say, "Ho, Shubin!" It was just like shifting into low gear on a motor vehicle.

The third was Danny-Boy and he was also special. He was a wicked dog, so mean that his eyes were red. Whenever we were travelling across country and he saw something dark along the trail, he would bite onto the harness, shake his head and growl. The rest of the team would get a surge of renewed energy and off they would go.

Terry was the fourth dog and he was the ears of the team. He was the first to sense any activity. He was black and white and his pointed ears would move to and fro, listening. The fifth dog was Tiny, but he wasn't, he was just a normal-sized dog; and the sixth was Samby who also had a mean streak.

The last dog was Gray and he knew when to pull opposite to the swing of the toboggan head.

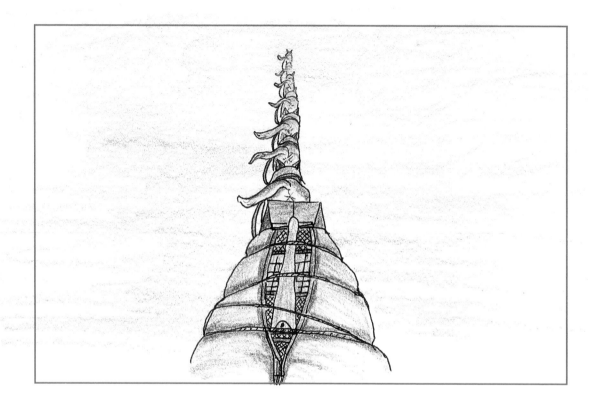

The dog team ran in a single file about forty feet in length. My lead dog was very special. Sometimes I would be travelling in a blizzard and, as the team stretched out, the lead dog, Puppy, would be out of sight. The howling wind and blowing snow would make it impossible to give commands. And then, at long last, after crossing a big lake, a dark streak of land would appear and Puppy would be right on the trail at the portage. Sometimes, I wanted to talk to him as I would to a human. That happens when you travel with dogs. When you travel in a blizzard you lose a sense of time and balance. You don't know whether you are going up...

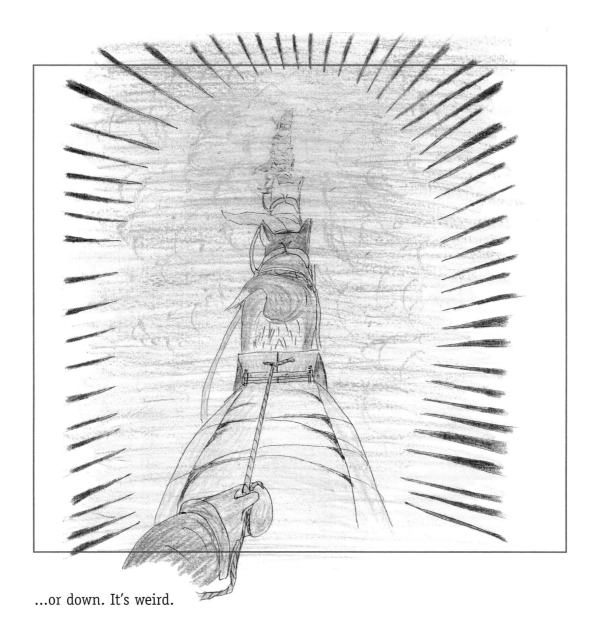

...or down. It's weird.

Caribou Hide

At the store in Colville Lake, I met Tom, the pilot for Aklak Air. He was hauling freight for the store from Fort Good Hope and had five trips to make. He said that he had seen about thirty caribou on the east side of the big island in Island Lake and he offered, if there was a hunter available, to fly the hunter out to the lake and then pick him up after his last trip. Bill, the store owner, said that there was a hunter right there and he meant me! I dropped my shopping for later.

I ran home to pick up my gear and hunting clothes: a single pair of pants, a jacket with a wolverine trimmed hood and a pair of beaver mitts. The rest of my gear was my grub bag, pack sack, axe, snowshoes and my .270 rifle and scope.

There was a blizzard blowing in from the east as we flew in to Island Lake. The herd of caribou was heading toward the south end of the island, so I told Tom to land on the lake at the north end of the island, and take off in that direction, too, in order to avoid spooking the herd.

The plane took off and I started walking toward the island in my snowshoes.
With the wind of the blizzard howling into my face, it was hard to see, so I
fastened up my hood, the wolverine trimming making it possible for me to face
into the blizzard.

I hurried to the island, trekking through about three feet of snow in my small trail snowshoes. I was looking for the highest ridge of the island. When I reached the ridge I could see where the caribou herd was, a hazy image of the herd. It was a big island and I headed for the south end following the tree line where the snow was softer.

The wind blowing through the trees made a sound like waves out on a lake as I came out onto the shore. I figured out where the caribou would come out: at the end of the point.

Before long, the lead caribou came into view. I waited until they all came out, then I shot the leader, then the last one. I kept doing that, to and fro. After I shot thirteen, I let the rest go.

I was happy, everything was going according to plan and I would have lots of time to butcher the caribou. So, first thing I should do, I thought to myself, is make a campfire and have something to eat. I found a leaning tree which would make a good shelter against the wind. After I had the fire crackling and spruce boughs spread for a mat, I put snow in the teapot and decided to butcher a small caribou for the ribs; ribs to roast by a campfire. I had a fantasy of nice fat ribs, sizzling. That was when I found out that my hunting knife was not in my pack sack. I had left it at home on the table.

I was dismayed; time was not in my favour. At all costs, I had to have the meat prepared for the airplane and the only tool available was my axe. So I began to file it down to a narrow taper. I wasn't hungry anymore and as soon as the axe was sharpened enough, I made haste to the butchering.

When I'd finished cutting up the thirteen caribou, I hauled the meat into two piles. Now I could roast the ribs. I knew the plane would be making its last trip to Colville Lake about that time, so I had a nice meal and began to prepare myself for the pick up.

The wind was so strong that the plane landed like a seagull; it hardly even skidded forwards. Leaving the engine running, the pilot told me that one of the ski struts was fractured and he couldn't take any passengers. "OK," I told him, "It's only eighteen miles to Colville Lake anyway."

I watched the plane take off. I thought to myself that I had to have a windbreaker to walk back with. A young caribou hide would be just right. I took a hide ashore to thaw out at the camp fire and then built another fire and cooked myself a hearty meal of ribs and tea. After the ribs and four cups of tea, I took the softened caribou hide and, while it was freezing again, formed it about my shoulders to protect me while I was walking. The cold wind of the blizzard was penetrating my single pair of pants; I would be walking with the wind on my right side. Because of the blizzard, it was getting dark very quickly. After year of travelling between Fort Good Hope and Colville Lake with a dog team, I knew where the trail would be at the shore. A traditional route was ploughed by the cat-train to Colville each year, but I would have to get ashore to find it even though I could only see a few yards ahead.

The wind was much stronger out in the middle of the lake, but the caribou hide windbreaker worked wonders and with that pressed into my side, I made it ashore and had no trouble finding the main trail. Walking along a stretch of cut-line, it was very dark and the wind among the trees added to the deafening sounds of the blizzard like waves in a big gale. Occasionally, I ran at a fast gait in my snowshoes; I had to try to make good time. The wind was strongest going over the mountain ridge toward Belot Lake, and it was no different as I went out onto that big lake. I was just walking with an inherent instinct.

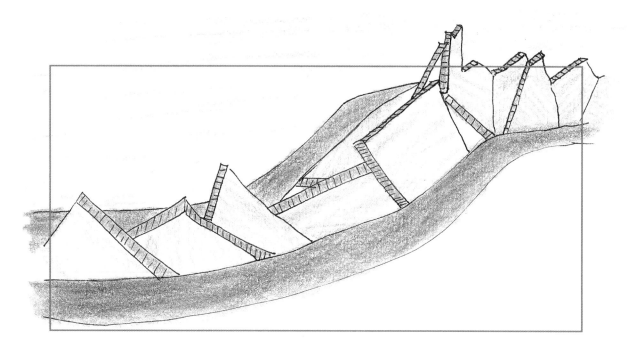

About fifteen or twenty minutes out onto Belot Lake, I saw a faint, dark streak in front of me. I struck a big wooden match and it briefly gave me enough light to see a reflection. Stepping back slowly, I realized that I was on a broken piece of ice. The dark streak was a pressure ridge. Every full moon the Lake responds to pressure and the ice comes together and then goes apart again. Every year it's about the same place.

I knew where the pressure ridge would go, it would run along the west bay of the lake and be too long a detour. I put the hide windbreaker back on my shoulders and headed back to Island Lake.

I was very tired when I arrived back at my campfire shelter. I made a fire in the old fire place and cooked myself a good meal. After I had eaten, I remembered what my Dad used to say, "If you sleep in caribou hides make sure there is enough room to come out in the morning. Once the hide freezes, you could be stuck in it."

I went out onto the lake and got two big hides. Thawing out the first hide, I lay on top of it on the ground where I chose to sleep. Because it was so cold it soon froze into my shape with the edges up and the hair inside. I thawed out the second hide and lay down with it over me, hair-side in; in no time it was frozen solid. Using my pack sack for a pillow I made myself comfortable and it was lights out for the night. With the blizzard howling outside, I fell into a deep slumber.

I awoke the next morning to a calm day. It was about forty below and the sky was clear and cold. I had prepared kindling for a fire the night before and so from where I was sleeping I lit the shavings and in no time the campfire was blazing.

As I was having tea, two hunters came across the lake from the west shore. I recognized them and they told me they were with a party of hunters from Fort Good Hope who had come out with dog teams to look for caribou. They were heading for Burning Snow Lake. They were amazed by my survival skills. I told them that the other nine caribou had gone into the bush at the southwest end of the lake, where the abandoned fuel drums were.

As I was waiting for someone from Colville Lake to come and look for me, I saw the two hunters going ashore and not too long after I heard nine shots.

Soon after, my friend John McNeely from Colville Lake, came by skidoo and picked me up. We took some meat back, too.